Janak Sapkota has the gift to look at things with a clear-sighted attentiveness. He has trained his eye to look intently, to look intelligently. He is a see-r, a visionary of the Real. Here he has created a body of work that is suffused with genius.

Cathal Ó Searcaigh

Janak Sapkota, from Nepal, is passionate about poetry, especially haiku, which he has been writing since 2002. He has won first place in numerous haiku contests, and has had his haiku and senryu published internationally in journals and magazines such as *The SHOp*, *Shamrock*, *Lishanu*, *Fri Haiku* and *Notes from the Gean*. While on a writing residency at Cló Ceardlann na gCnoc in Ireland, he published *Full Moon* (2010). His most recent collections include *Whisper of Pines: Cogar na nGúiseanna* (2011) and *A Firefly Lights the Page: Tulikärpänen valaisee sivun* (2012). In between poetry books, Janak has earned a PhD in natural sciences from the University of Fribourg, Switzerland. He now resides in Austria, where he continues to mix science with 17-syllable poetry.

long days of rain
Janak Sapkota

Ⓟ **Onslaught** South Asia Series **no 1**

Published in Oxford by The Onslaught Press
11 Ridley Road, OX4 2QJ
1 February 2017

Haiku © 2017 **Janak Sapkota**

Cover design (including a detail from *Evening View of Kiribata in Rain at Akasaka* by Hiroshige II), illustrations, and this edition © 2017 **Mathew Staunton**

Janak Sapkota asserts his moral right to be identified as the author of this book

All rights reserved. No part of this publication may be reproduced, stored in a retrieval system, or transmitted, in any form or by any means, electronic, mechanical, photocopying, recording, or otherwise, without the prior permission in writing of the publisher, or as expressly permitted by law, or under terms agreed with the appropriate reprographics rights organization

ISBN: 978-1-912111-71-8

Typeset in Akira Kobayashi's **Din Next**
Designed & edited by **Mathew Staunton**

Printed & bound by Lightning Source

to my loving grandmother

a busy ant
    loses its way
among my haiku

long days of rain—
    the gurgle of frogs ripens
the little rice field

picking words for a poem
there's a power cut
a firefly lights the page

in the garden, a marigold
makes eyes at
a wild bee

rain

    ants gather
   under a mushroom

ploughing the rice field—
   birds
squabble over earthworms

reading a poem out aloud
   I pause in the field—

grasshoppers take up the words

monsoon rain—
    walking by the dump
    smell of jasmine

geese by the lake
waterlilies
such whiteness

old man dozes in the sun—
    withering flower
   in a clay pot

in the ritzy garden
   even the bees
      drink coca-cola

in the gale
    a tree spreads its shadow
over the stream

a scattering
    of magnolia blossoms—
        windswept clouds

in the darkening rain
   a peacock
lights up the morning

thinking it's daylight
    a bee searches for flowers
around a table lamp

autumn moon—
   the pipal tree washed
     with swathes of gold

it slowly fades—
    the shadow of a ladybird
in the gutter

rainy afternoon
   the drainpipes gurgle
    breathlessly

walking through
   withered grass
a dream of grasshoppers

living near woods
   no need of an alarm—
      cuckoos

this cold night
on the mountaintop, even the silence
becomes ice

in the lotus pool
    the moon sits
in the lotus position

heavy rain
    a crow and a sparrow
        share the window ledge

no sheep of his in that flock—

   a shepherd peers
   at the clouds

in the winter snow
    a cow remembers
        chewing its cud

the plop

of wild berries in the river
delights the otter

a downpour of rain
    then a mist through the village—
the reek of goats

a tree heavy with snow—
a sunbeam
lightens its load

white chrysanthemums—

even the breeze
treats them gently

after heavy rain
   a white cloud glows
waiting to be admired

at the temple gate
   a dragon fly
       waits for the blessing

snow in the mountain—
the gurgle of tea
thaws the silence

ash from the ghat—
   in the moonlight, a shadow
crosses the river

on a broken street lamp
    a firefly
alights

I wake up early
with a haiku on my mind—

    a dawn cuckoo

after the rain, a mosquito
    roams at sunlight
feverishly

a sudden flash
walking on snow

a peacock

in the tree branch
   a hanging nest
warbles in the wind

rain clouds over Phulchoki
    the pathway
        is thronged with snails

a wooden chair
   I hear the groan of a tree
      as I sit down

a sparrow waits
   for me to be still
then crosses the street

steam of my boiling tea
   hides the wintry moon
in the window

spring snow
    only bird tracks
show the way

birthday
that lovely present
the bright sky

rain clouds over Kathmandu
on a grey path
I ascend to the sky

sing out your heart, cicada
   surely, someone
will pass

winter morning chill—
  red rose
    glows in the room

whispering pines
walking through them

    I hear secrets

on a windy night
   the candle in the room
tries to be still

butterfly—

it flutters to remind
her eyelashes

a burning candle—
    the shivering heart
longs for its flame

stroke of luck—
lodged in my wallet

a strand of her hair

inside the tomb—
   it feels safe enough
      to whisper a secret

the musty smell
   of an old cupboard—
your parting kiss

deep in the night
 the scent of lavender

you at my door

the swell of her breast
she breathes me
in and out

in the icy night
    your footsteps sadly
crunch past my door

I open the window
dogs bark in the distance—

alone with stars

lonely path—

only the midnight owl
for company

a glass of water
between the gulps
you were raped

full moon
　　walking through a forest
why should I fear

thinking of death
　my teacup slips
　　and breaks

a ripple of light—
    in the silence a rose
unfold its petals

full moon
    the old woman at the temple
bays at god

in the outdoor cafe
    momos are garnished
      with birdsong

the rickshaw boy
    waiting for a customer
falls asleep

the foreign preacher—
    in his bag even closed
a bible rants

gracefully
the cobbler spreads out his shop
in the dead-end street

in tears—
    a sick child
stares at the rain

in the grim street
   a dog growls
at the sunset

after peering at the sunset
   grandmother
hurries to her mirror

nobody comes to see her

but a fern adorns
her tombstone

weary of his wife
    he hugs the full moon
in the riverbed

refugee camp
the full moon gleams

on empty plates

the ants are carrying
    much more than they can
in this famished land

on the battlefield
   between the bones

weeds

an open grave
   a bleached bone
glows in the moonlight

an evening of gunfire
   a wild goose
searches for its mate

early morning dew—

in a Baghdad street
    blood glistens on a tree

on the dusty wall, the old soldier
looks at his war medals
festooned with spider webs

a black dog
    challenges a beggar
in a lonely street

the little girl
    puts a nappy
on the blooming flower

inside a bus
    this housefly knows nothing
       of where it is going

a blackboard—
    I submit to the words of others
to lighten the darkness

so bored—
I read my book
again and again

a pair of white doves—
   alight on the eyes
of the sleeping Buddha

autumn evening—
a lone swallow
shapes the wind

fireworks—
then the silence
of falling stars

alpine meadow
   a saffron flower
      and a Hindu sadhu

no fish
just dry leaves
in the summer lake

deserted summer—
a pigeon peeks
at shrunken cherries

no way out
   a housefly hums
      as I stand by

a halo
    of corn silk
        for her bald father

no traffic signals
    just the white lines
of flying herons

weightlessness—
   the full moon
      on a butterfly's wing

stillness—
deep in the forest

a cicada

late summer
    although the village is deserted
        a hibiscus keeps blooming

a couple camping—
      next to the dim candle
a firefly

a girl
    next to the snowman
        snow piles up on her hat

on the mountain
   a skylark and its echo
         ascends

a clear lake
    oh! a camellia—
on the moonless night

summer—
withered in the field
    a scarecrow

midsummer
 mimicking herself
  cuckoo . . . . . cuckoo

autumn—
    same old trees
        bare and lifeless

the battlefield
is history—
tulips bloom

lost myself
        looking for temples
in the misty slopes

o wind, did you bring me
   a foggy blanket
        on this mountaintop?

midsummer
on a straw hat
    freshly picked flowers

day by day
   an old oak falls—
      those busy termites

Some of the haiku in this edition were originally published in *Winter Light* (Gortahork: Cló Ceardlann na gCnoc, 2004), *Lights Along The Road* (Kathmandu: Bamboo Press, 2005), *Full Moon* (Gortahork: Cló Ceardlann na gCnoc, 2010), *Whisper of Pines: Cogar na nGiúiseanna* (Dublin: Original Writing, 2011) and *A Firefly Lights the Page: Tulikärpänen valaisee sivun* (Tampere: SanaSato, 2012).

other haiku titles from The Onslaught Press:

Sneachta (2016) Gabriel Rosenstock

Tea wi the Abbot (2016) Scots haiku by John McDonald
with transcreations in Irish by Gabriel Rosenstock

Judgement Day (2016) Gabriel Rosenstock

Antlered Stag of Dawn (2015) Gabriel Rosenstock,
with translations by Mariko Sumikura & John McDonald

behind the yew hedge (2015) Mathew Staunton & Gabriel Rosenstock

and some of our poetry titles:

ident (2016) Alan John Stubbs

the lightbulb has stigmata (2016) Helen Fletcher

Out of the Wilderness (2016) by Cathal Ó Searcaigh
with an introduction and translations by Gabriel Rosenstock

You Found a Beating Heart (2016) Nisha Bhakoo

I Wanna Make Jazz to You (2016) Moe Seager

We Want Everything (2016) Moe Seager

to kingdom come (2016) edited by Rethabile Masilo

The Lost Box of Eyes (2016) Alan John Stubbs

Bumper Cars (2015) Athol Williams

Waslap (2015) Rethabile Masilo

Aistear Anama (2014) Tadhg Ó Caoinleáin

for the children of Gaza (2014)
edited by Mathew Staunton & Rethabile Masilo

Poison Trees (2014) Philippe Saltel & Mathew Staunton

www.ingramcontent.com/pod-product-compliance
Lightning Source LLC
LaVergne TN
LVHW011424080426
835512LV00005B/252